583
Sel   Selsam, Millicent E

     Milkweed

	DATE DUE		

MILKWEED

Millicent E. Selsam

photographs by Jerome Wexler

William Morrow & Company   New York 1967

By the Same Author

ANIMALS AS PARENTS

THE COURTSHIP OF ANIMALS

HOW ANIMALS LIVE TOGETHER

HOW TO GROW HOUSE PLANTS

THE LANGUAGE OF ANIMALS

MICROBES AT WORK

PLANTS THAT HEAL

PLANTS THAT MOVE

THE PLANTS WE EAT

PLAY WITH PLANTS

PLAY WITH SEEDS

PLAY WITH TREES

UNDERWATER ZOOS

HOW ANIMALS TELL TIME

Published simultaneously in Canada by
George J. McLeod Limited, Toronto.
Printed in the United States of America.
Library of Congress Catalog Card Number 67-21733

••

The photographs on pages 21, 42, and 47 are by
Hal Harrison, Jeanne White, and Bernard Gluck respectively
from the National Audubon Society.

The author and photographer thank
Mr. Noel H. Holmgren,
associated with the
New York Botanical Garden,
for checking the text
and photographs of this book.

Did you ever blow on a milkweed pod as this boy is doing? He is watching the seeds sail away in the air.

The seeds are all over his face. But they can't grow there.

Each seed has silky white hairs, which act as a parachute. The wind carries the seed through the air. When the seed hits a tree or a fence or a stone wall, it separates from its parachute and falls to the ground.

If the soil is wet, the seed will sprout. Here a milkweed plant has started to grow from the seed. The cover of the seed hasn't fallen off the young plant yet.

The milkweed plant is growing bigger.

The leaves open in pairs.

The plant keeps getting bigger.

Soon you can see flower buds.

When the flower buds grow bigger, you can see that they are grouped in clusters. Count the number of clusters on a plant.

Each cluster has more than fifty flowers.

As the buds open, the flower petals fall
back.

Many buds are opening.

Here the flower is fully opened. It is strangely different from an ordinary and simple kind of flower.

The simple flower usually has a ring of stamens around a pistil in the center. There may be one or many pistils.

daffodil

The stamens have little bags of pollen grains on the top. If you touch the pollen with your finger, you will see that it looks like yellow dust. Sometimes pollen has a different color like brown or purple.

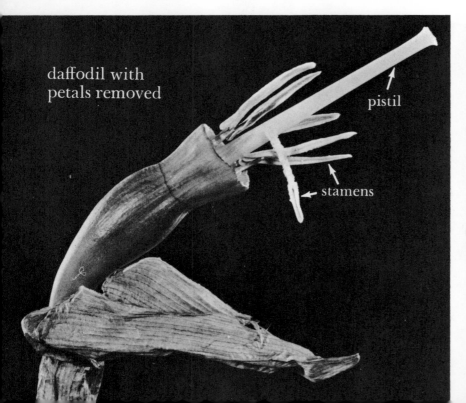

daffodil with petals removed

pistil

stamens

close-up of pollen bag

The pistil in the center is important, because at the bottom of it you can find ovules, or seeds-to-be.

They become seeds only if they are fertilized, or joined, by the contents of a pollen grain.

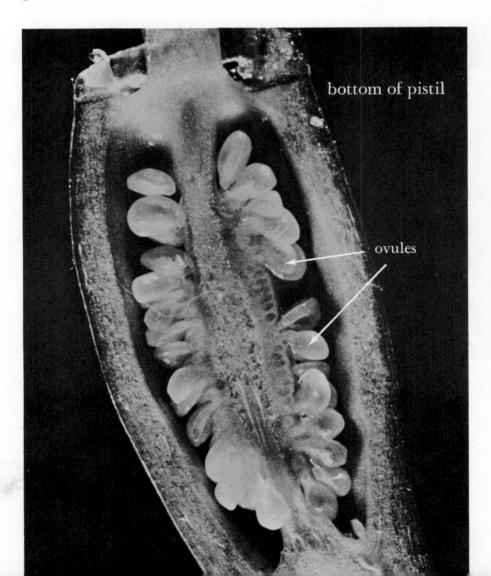

bottom of pistil

ovules

Wind may carry pollen from flower to flower.

Birds may carry pollen from flower to flower.

Insects may carry pollen from flower to flower.

Here is the milkweed flower again.

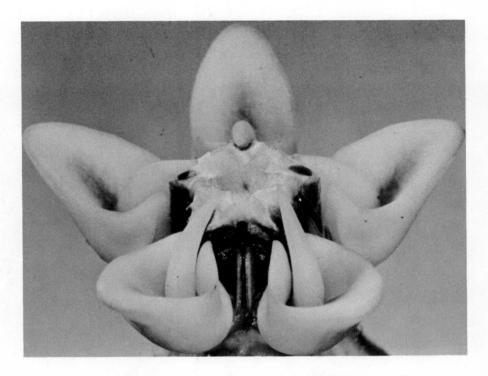

After the petals have folded back, you can see parts that look like petals, but are really cups containing nectar, the sweet juice of flowers. There are five nectar cups. Each has a little horn, which curves in toward the center of the flower.

On a warm day in July you can see a crowd of insects buzzing around each milk-weed plant. The color of the flowers and their sweet smell attract them.

The insects are trying to suck the nectar.
But doing so is not easy. All parts of the
flower are smooth and slippery. The flower
bends under the weight of the insect.

The only way an insect can keep from slipping is to put its feet into the slits between the nectar cups. You can see a slit in the center of the picture. Notice the shiny black thing at the top of the slit.

slit

There are five such slits in the flower.

As the insect tries to take hold, it moves its feet from one end of the slit to the other. The shiny black thing at the top is split like a clamp. The insect's feet get wedged into it.

When an insect struggles to get free of the flower it pulls. Out comes the black clip attached to its foot. Two yellow bags of pollen hang from the clip.

Sometimes several feet get caught in the slits at the same time, and the insect pulls out a few pairs of pollen bags.

The pollen is not powdery like ordinary pollen. It is waxy and sticks together in the small pear-shaped packages you see here. They are being held on the point of a straight pin.

Sometimes the bees or flies or butterflies that visit the milkweed flowers are not strong enough to pull away, and they are trapped.

Here you can see a fly caught in a flower.

An insect that has pollen bags on its feet goes to another flower. Now its feet holding the pollen bags again slip into the slit of the flower. The insect moves its foot from one end of the slit to the other. This time the pollen bags break off. They are left in the slit.

The pollen grains still have to reach the ovules at the bottom of the pistil. At the back of the slit there is a sugary liquid in which pollen grains can grow. The pollen grains push out tubes sideways, into the stalk of the pistil, and then grow down to the bottom, where the ovules are. The contents of each pollen tube join with an ovule.

The ovules are fertilized and now will change into seeds.

The bottom of the pistil, the ovary, becomes a pod.

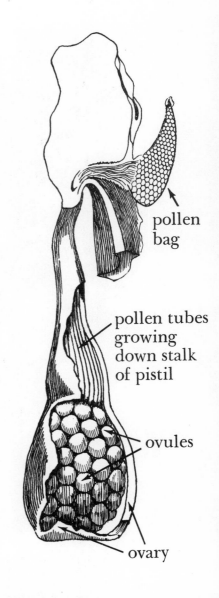

pollen bag

pollen tubes growing down stalk of pistil

ovules

ovary

The flowers are dying. Most of them are not fertilized, because pollination is very difficult. Many pollen bags are not put into the slits. The flowers that are not fertilized wither and fall to the ground.

But you can find pods in each cluster.

pod

From the whole cluster of flowers only three pods are developing.

As the pods get bigger, they turn up and point their tips toward the sky. When fall comes, the leaves dry up and fall off.

The pods remain high up on the tall stems.

In each pod you can see hundreds of brown seeds overlapping each other like shingles on a roof.

A few pods are enough to spread the milkweed far and wide, because each pod is packed so fully with seeds.

a cut-open pod

a pod opening by itself

Now you can see the tuft of silky hairs attached to each seed. The wind is pulling them out of the pod.

Many pods are open, and many seeds are leaving the pods.

Now the seeds fly through the air. Soon they fall to the ground.

Next spring there will be many new milkweed plants.

The old milkweed plant from which the seeds have come dies down. But under the ground there are living roots, and next spring they will send up new shoots. This kind of plant is called a perennial, because it stays alive from year to year.

The milkweed plant is useful.

People used to use the silky hairs to stuff pillows. You can stuff a doll's mattress or pillow with them.

During World War II milkweed seed pods were collected, and the silky hairs were used in life preservers. Three and a half pounds of silky hairs kept a man afloat for three days.

Each silky hair is a hollow tube coated with wax. Water cannot enter easily.

You can pull the fibers out of the milk-weed stem and use them to tie things together. American Indians used the fibers to make cloth.

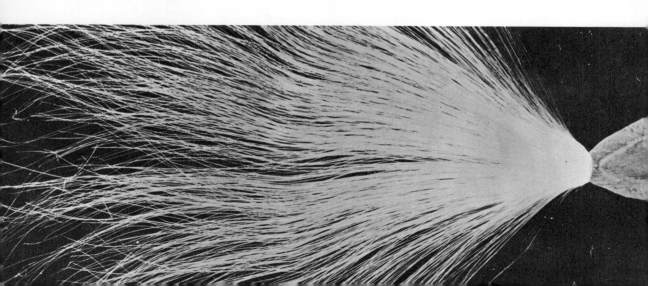

If you break any part of the plant, a milky fluid oozes out.

Put some of the milky juice on your thumb and index finger. Let it dry. Then touch your fingers together and move them apart slowly. The dried milky juice is sticky and acts like rubber cement. Try using it as a paste.

Birds and insects use the milkweed plant too. We have seen how bees, butterflies, beetles, wasps, and flies live on its nectar.

The caterpillar of the monarch butterfly feeds on milkweed leaves.

Next time you see milkweed, think of all the things that make it such a remarkable plant.

CONCORD OXBOW SCHOOL